Our Abba

Praying the Lord's Prayer
So It Comes Alive
In Us

James E. Miller

WILLOWGREEN®

To Bernie, of course

Book design by Katherine Misegades
Cover photograph by James E. Miller

Credit
The quotation on page 29 is from *Our Heavenly Father: Sermons on the Lord's Prayer* by Helmut Thielicke, Lutterworth Press, Cambridge, U.K. 1988.

WILL🌿WGREEN®
10351 Dawson's Creek Boulevard, Suite B
Fort Wayne, Indiana 46825
260.490.2222
www.willowgreen.com

ISBN 978-1-885933-18-8

The Lord's Prayer

Our Father who art in heaven,
Hallowed be thy name.
Thy kingdom come,
Thy will be done,
On earth as it is in heaven.
Give us this day our daily bread;
And forgive us our debts,
As we forgive our debtors.
And lead us not into temptation,
But deliver us from evil.
For thine is the kingdom,
and the power,
and the glory forever.
Amen.

This version is based mostly upon its appearance in *The Gospel According to Matthew*. Other versions are also in use today, as these pages will make clear.

Foreword

"You'd be surprised how many weeks of the year have Sundays in them." I used to say that occasionally when I was the sole minister of a Protestant congregation. Coming up with meaningful, relevant sermons week after week took a lot of work, especially on top of the many other responsibilities most ministers carry. I can still remember, thirty years later, the pressure I felt.

So when Peace United Church of Christ in Fort Wayne, Indiana announced they were giving their pastor a three-month sabbatical, so that she could recharge herself, naturally I was supportive. Realizing there weren't extra funds to provide pulpit supply in her absence, and wanting to do what I could to ease the way for this dedicated minister (who happens to double as my daughter), I volunteered to lead worship and preach four Sundays in a row. After some thought, I settled on the topic of the Lord's Prayer. I had never done this topic in depth, so it seemed about time that I did.

My sermons usually lumber along for fifteen to eighteen minutes, so that meant I had an hour to an hour and a quarter, tops, to tell a sanctuary full of people all they needed to know about the most important prayer in all Christendom. I imagined that, along the way, I'd want to throw in a few stories, raise a few questions, reveal a couple of surprising facts, and toss out a handful of personal observations.

It didn't take long to realize that the task I had set for myself would be impossible to fulfill. I could not, within that limited timeframe, do it all. I could not detail the historical context, explore fully this prayer's unusual structure, explain the nuances of the three languages involved, delve line by line into each of the prayer's phrases, while regularly stepping back and treating this lovely piece of scripture for what it is—a beautiful and honest prayer that's an authentic expression of the soul and heart of Jesus.

Eventually, I let myself off the hook. I decided I'd casually preach the four allotted sermons without rushing and without cramming each one too full. I gave myself that freedom after determining that I'd write down in book form some of the additional things I did not have time to say from the pulpit. I'd publish this manuscript and pass it out to the congregation as a gift on that last Sunday. That's what you now hold in your hands.

Let's be honest: thousands of scholarly and inspirational books and articles have been written through the centuries by a vast number of theologians and authors, most all of them more knowledgeable than I. What can I do in sixty-four short pages that will make the printing of this book worthwhile?

Perhaps only this: leave a trace of my genuine awe for this beautiful prayer, first spoken by an amazingly spiritual man. It is my goal to do this in a way that addresses the reader's heart and soul as well as their mind, their memory, and their hope.

If this should happen, if only partially and fitfully, I will have done what I could. Should you yourself come away enriched, if only a bit, then this venerable prayer will have done its lofty work one more time.

True Story

Helmut Thielicke pursued his career as a German theologian at a time when Adolph Hitler was rising to power. One of Hitler's authoritarian moves was to arrange the creation of a single national church, overseen by an Imperial Bishop, who reported directly to the führer. This church submissively went along with Hitler's various pronouncements, including the repugnant notion of the natural superiority of the Aryan race.

Dr. Thielicke, strongly opposed to such ideas, joined the Confessing Church—an underground resistance movement opposed to the Nazi propaganda machine. As punishment for his resistance, Thielicke, who was a pastor as well as a professor, was exiled to a tiny parish in the middle of nowhere, and forbidden to travel, so that hardly anyone could hear him speak his thoughts.

In 1943, inexplicably, he was allowed to move to the modest city of Stuttgart, and permitted to speak in the cathedral there, though never on Sunday mornings. These once-a-week evening programs could not be billed as worship services, and yet his talks were nothing less than sermons—powerful sermons.

People turned out to hear him, three thousand at a time, with standing room only. He spoke to people whose husbands and fathers and sons had died as German soldiers, far away, many left behind in mass graves. He spoke to people whose spouses and children and grandchildren and friends had been injured or killed by the Allied bombings. While he was there, the Stuttgart city center was leveled and a large number of homes destroyed.

In 1944, when things seemed at their worst, and their beautiful cathedral had been totally demolished by bombs, Dr. Thielicke decided to preach a series of sermons in various large halls around the city. He wanted to comfort, strengthen, and challenge the people of Stuttgart as they went through those chaotic and frightening times. So that's what he did. The subject of this sermon series that people flocked to hear—sometimes walking for several miles because public transportation no longer existed and roads lay in ruins everywhere—the subject he chose was the Lord's Prayer.

Shaken by grief and fear, the Lord's Prayer.

Stunned by the atrocities of their own government, the Lord's Prayer.

Immobilized by their terribly uncertain future, as a city, as a nation, even as a world, the Lord's Prayer.

His sermons were deemed revolutionary enough they could not be printed or published. So after each preaching, he would detail the essence of what he had just said to a roomful of two hundred stenographers, each of whom would then make ten handwritten copies to be passed out to others, and each of these made ten more copies, on and on.

It's difficult for us to appreciate the fact that not that many years ago a simple prayer inspired by an itinerant Galilean prophet could, first, so rile the authorities and, second, create such a strong positive response among so many people. These people took their own risks in going to hear what this kind, learned theologian had to say. They sat in deep silence and listened to words about a prayer they had known by heart from their very early days. It was such a simple prayer, made up mostly of very common words. Yet it was a strangely transformative prayer as he explained it to them.

The Lord's Prayer, of course, has made its way into ever so many other gatherings down through the years. It's been a part of large religious feasts and fancy royal coronations. It's equally fitting in small country churches and majestic cathedrals and modern chapels, in hospitals and workplaces and fields of combat. It appears at weddings, at funerals, at bedsides, at mealtimes, in quiet times. It suits equally the most public of venues and the most private of personal experiences. There is no place on earth, no time whether consequential or inconsequential, no human experience whether of joy or sorrow or anything in between, in which this prayer is not at home.

The Lord's Prayer has been spoken and sung and whispered in unending succession from the time it was first revealed, so that it can do its enlarging, healing, and transforming work everywhere it is breathed. This is the prayer we turn to today, searching for the wisdom, the direction, and the hope it can bring to us in our individual lives, our collective communities, and our fractured world.

Draw closer.

Get better acquainted with the Lord's Prayer. Pray it quietly each morning upon awakening. Whisper it to yourself before going to sleep each night. Pray it intermittently through the day as it feels natural. See what happens.

The Lord's Prayer may be committed to memory quickly,
but it is slowly learnt by heart.

FREDERICK DENISON MAURICE

I felt it better to speak to God
than about God.

THERESE OF LISIEUX

To this day I am still nursing myself
on the Lord's Prayer like a child,
and I am still eating and drinking of it
like an old man without getting bored with it.

MARTIN LUTHER

I used to think the Lord's Prayer was a short prayer;
but as I live longer, and see more of life,
I begin to believe there is no such thing
as getting through it.
If a person, in praying that prayer,
were to be stopped by every word
until one had thoroughly prayed it,
it would take one a lifetime.

HENRY WARD BEECHER

Beginnings

The story of the life of Jesus is told four times in the New Testament. The earliest version, written around 65 to 70 AD, is The Gospel According to Mark. It contains no mention of the Lord's Prayer. Neither does the last in the series, The Gospel According to John, probably written in the 90s AD.

The other two gospels, Matthew and Luke, composed most likely during the 80s, *do* contain what has come to be called the Lord's Prayer. They each report that Jesus suggested specific words for how his followers should pray. However, these two accounts of what was said and how it was said do not agree with each other.

According to Luke, Jesus had been praying in a place where he was presumably alone. When he stopped his praying, one of his disciples approached him and said, "Lord, teach us to pray." It sounded as much like a demand as a request.

This unnamed disciple's words are noteworthy on two counts. First, as observant Jews, the disciples already knew about prayer. They understood that all adult males were expected to face toward Jerusalem three times a day and pray. They were aware of prayer spoken in public worship in synagogues.

The second thing of note is the qualifying remark this disciple tacked on: "Lord, teach us to pray as John taught his disciples." John, of course, is John the Baptist. Both Jesus and John were contemporaneous prophetic figures who attracted followers. John was known to be the more ascetic one, and the one more driven to resist the Roman authorities. From this account it appears there was something attractive about the specific instructions John provided his followers. The disciples of Jesus wanted something similar, for their own comfort level if for no other reason.

According to the story in Luke, Jesus responded to the disciple by launching right in, "When you pray, say…" and then he told them exactly what to say:

> Father, hallowed be thy name.
>
> Thy kingdom come.
>
> Give us each day our daily bread;
>
> and forgive us our sins, for we ourselves forgive every one who
>> is indebted to us;
>
> and lead us not into temptation.

As the words of this short prayer hung in the air, Jesus started telling a story built around the theme of "ask and it will be given you." Perhaps Luke is suggesting that's the message behind this prayer. Whatever Luke's purpose, he never revisited this prayer.

When we look at how Matthew deals with the way Jesus first revealed the Lord's Prayer, we are met with an entirely different story. Chapters 5, 6, and 7 in Matthew contain the Sermon on the Mount. It's introduced with these words: "Seeing the crowds, he went up on the mountain, and when he sat down his disciples came to him. And he opened his mouth and taught them,…" At first reading, "them" seems to refer to his disciples. As the sermon concludes, however, in 7:28, we are told, "And when Jesus finished these sayings, the crowds were astonished at his teaching,…" This suggests that there were many more than just the disciples to whom Jesus spoke that day.

Whoever heard his words, in the middle of this sermon Jesus gave some advice about prayer in general. "When you pray, go into your room and shut the door." "Do not heap up empty phrases as the Gentiles do." Then he makes his advice more specific: "Pray then like this:". The words that come out of his mouth are a longer version of the Lord's Prayer:

> *Our Father who art in heaven,*
>
> *Hallowed be thy name.*
>
> *Thy kingdom come.*
>
> *Thy will be done, on earth as it is in heaven.*
>
> *Give us this day our daily bread;*
>
> *And forgive us our debts,*
>
> > *As we also have forgiven our debtors.*
>
> *And lead us not into temptation,*
>
> *But deliver us from evil.*

The prayer ends there, and Jesus moved immediately to talk about forgiveness and fasting and other suggestions for how to live one's life.

As we prepare to look more closely at the words Jesus supplied, which version shall we use? Both renditions sound authentic to the voice of Jesus. They unfold in a similar order. For our purposes here, we'll go with what Matthew has passed on. It's more commonly accepted in congregations around the world. I propose that's as good a reason as any.

Practice pausing.

Take longer than normal to say the Lord's Prayer. Pause at the end of every phrase, giving yourself plenty of time with each word. Don't think. Just be soulfully quiet. Take at least five minutes. Work your way up to ten.

The Lord's Prayer is the quintessence of prayer.

DIETRICH BONHOEFFER

Prayer is the breathing of the soul.

JOHN OF CRONSTADT

Prayer oneth the soul to God.

JULIAN OF NORWICH

We and God have business with each other;
and in opening ourselves to God's influence
our deepest destiny is fulfilled.

WILLIAM JAMES

The hope on which my prayer rests
is in the fact that it is God who wants it.
And if I go to keep the appointment
it is because God is already there waiting for me.

CARLO CARRETTO

Form

Before looking into the individual parts of the prayer Jesus composed—the *only* prayer he composed for others as far as we know—let's look at the overall structure of his composition. The Lord's Prayer is distinctly, if somewhat mysteriously, designed.

The Lord's Prayer is formed of Jewish concepts.

Jesus spoke plainly the words he wanted his followers to use. He did not propose some general ideas for what to pray. He did not offer options. He said, in effect, "Speak exactly these phrases and keep them in this order."

The words he strung together were not all that new to his listeners' ears. Many Jewish scriptures contained references to God's name, God's kingdom, and God's will. Stories highlighting the giving or sharing of bread were common. The theme of forgiveness was woven throughout many Hebrew scriptures. Indeed, one might imagine that some of the first recipients of this prayer may have asked themselves, "Is that all? Haven't we heard much of this somewhere before?"

We do not know the response of Jesus's disciples or his other followers. The gospel writer turns immediately to other thoughts that Jesus had on his mind. We *do* know that in his prayer Jesus chose to call upon traditional language and established ideas—mostly.

Whatever words he chose, Jesus wanted to breathe new life into these ideas that he fashioned into prayer. And, as we shall see, he did.

The Lord's Prayer is formed of and rooted in a distant language, or more accurately, languages.

Jesus never spoke the words we use today when we speak his prayer. English did not come into being until over fourteen centuries years after he died. When first committed to writing, the gospels were inscribed in Greek. It's unclear how much of that language Jesus understood himself, for his native tongue was Aramaic, which had been the dominant language in that part of the world for centuries.

With its own unique alphabet and lettering that moves from right to left, with its complex and fluid sounds that are not heard in either Greek or English, Aramaic seems very distant from what we're used to hearing or speaking. It's from another world.

Unfortunately, the prayer that Jesus offered in Aramaic was not preserved in that language. Some individual Aramaic words and phrases attributed to Jesus have been placed in the New Testament, but not many. Scholars recently have been working backward, making educated guesses in an attempt to translate the Lord's Prayer into its original words and sounds. A tentative consensus is gradually growing as to the words Jesus actually used when he delivered that gift of a prayer.

The Lord's Prayer has a well-ordered form.

It begins with a communication to the One who is being addressed, by name. There follow two sets of petitions, each set with its own theme. The first group of petitions, sometimes called the "thou petitions," three in number, has to do ostensibly with the Divine. The second set, sometimes called the "we petitions," focuses on the human dimension. This second group is counted as either three or four, depending on who's counting. Some assert that the last sentence that begins, "And lead us not into temptation..." contains two separate thoughts. Others maintain that this sentence is a single related thought. For our purposes here, we'll go with the structure of three—three thou petitions which build upon one another, and three we petitions which likewise show a progression in thought.

The prayer ends, in our modern version, with a doxology, which was added by the church some years after Jesus died. Not all Christian groups, however, include this as an ending.

The Lord's Prayer is a well-constructed, concise, eloquent expression of what Jesus thought, stood for, and dreamed of. One can sense a deep spiritual impulse at work.

Let's turn now to the individual lines of this great prayer—sometimes called The Greatest Prayer—so we can understand as clearly as possible what Jesus said, what he intended, and what he wanted all who follow him to know and to do.

Improvise.

Say the Lord's Prayer, stopping just before "For thine is..." Then pray whatever is on your mind and heart. Just be yourself. Use normal language. Conclude by saying the Prayer again, all the way through. Turn this into a regular practice.

17

The Prayer

When you pray,
rather let your heart be without words
than your words be without heart.

JOHN BUNYAN

Talk to God as you would talk
to your very best friend.
Tell the Holy One everything.

NACHMAN OF BRESLOV

Certain thoughts are prayers.
There are moments when,
whatever the attitude of the body,
the soul is on its knees.

VICTOR HUGO

I have made it a practice of saying the Lord's Prayer
through once each morning with absolute attention.
If during the recitation my attention wanders
or goes to sleep, in the minutest degree,
I begin again until I have once succeeded
in going through it with absolutely pure attention.

SIMONE WEIL

Father

In his book on the Lord's Prayer, William Carl writes about what it means to address God by offering an analogy. He refers to Dr. George Buttrick, for thirty years the minister at Madison Avenue Presbyterian Church in New York City and deemed one of the most important preachers in the twentieth century. Carl said that he was such an inspiring and powerful figure that no one could imagine calling him anything but "Dr. Buttrick." If someone asked, "What's his first name?" Carl reported the reply was "Dr."

I understand that. I was 22 and in my first year at Garrett Theological Seminary when I needed some extra money to replace the brakes on my aging Volkswagen. On a help wanted bulletin board I came across this notice: "Address our family's 800 Christmas cards. Must have excellent handwriting." I called the phone number and was given a time to appear at a couple's home. Once there, I was interviewed and then was carefully watched as I addressed two envelopes with a black fountain pen. I passed inspection.

That was the evening I first met Dr. and Mrs. Buttrick. At the age of 75 he had been named professor of homiletics at Garrett. He was an imposing man with a deep, resonant voice that could easily sound stern. He had eyes that seemed to pierce you. For a number of evenings that December I sat at the Buttrick's massive dining room table, carefully doing my work, almost afraid to make a noise. I could overhear the famous man in his library next door, talking on the phone, speaking with visitors, conversing with his wife. I became aware that even she referred to him as "Dr."

What William Carl wrote in his book and what I experienced in that wood-paneled dining room were the same: a small taste of what it could feel like to be in the presence of someone with a formidable bearing, someone before whom you could feel small, whether that's their intention or not. How do you address them? What do you say to them?

People who spent time around Jesus had similar wonderings. How do you address Someone as formidable as the Creator of the entire universe?

In the earliest days God was thought to be unapproachable and unreachable, far beyond the possibility of any human connection. God was so holy that one dare not even speak God's name. In the Old Testament God came to be principally identified as Yahweh. Over the course of time names were substituted that represented God as a supremely powerful ruler: Adonai and El Shaddai. Later God was referred to as King and Lord, among other names. Always these names carried the connotation of God's being very distant, very removed.

And then the next thing people knew, Jesus started calling God "Father." While that name had been used for God a handful of times in the Old Testament, it was always in the context of God as the father of a people, a land—Israel. There was no hint of one individual being able to relate closely to one God. Jesus did something radically new—he made that personal, immediate connection central to his practice of prayer.

The manner in which Jesus begins what has come to be called the Lord's Prayer would have been shocking to those around him. Speaking in his native tongue, Jesus chose the Aramaic word

22

Daddy ?

abba. It's a common word, used in every household—*abba*, dearest father.

Some have suggested that *abba* is best translated "daddy," but that's not the case. Three other Aramaic words (*abi*, *baba*, and *babi*) suggest that more child-like language. *Abba* suggests the special closeness of a caring parental figure that carries with it a degree of respect as well as a trust that has been earned. In calling God *abba*, Jesus melded the two: a majestic, omnipotent God with an accessible, loving God—in other words, a "Father who art in heaven."

God's home is heaven, a realm beyond all space and time. *heaven* From this unimaginably expansive space, God chooses to become available to human beings, prepared to engage in an inexplicable and surprising intimacy. Who could have known this kind of a relationship was even possible? One person did.

Just as Jesus created a transformative effect in our concept of the nature of God with the second word of his prayer, he did something equally transformative with that first word—"our." He begins by pronouncing, "*Our* Father." He does not say, "My Father" in the sense of "My (Jesus's) Father." He says in effect, "Feel free to address your prayer to the God who is the Father of us all. This God is equally your God as well as *my* God."

Jesus wanted to offer his followers what he had already experienced—a real closeness to God. One need not grovel, or act like a slave or a servant before God. With Jesus's lead, one can confidently and comfortably open one's mouth or one's mind and say, "dearest Father."

Another dimension of saying "*our* Father" is that the Lord's Prayer is intentionally and unquestionably always more than a private prayer. It is always prayed in community, even when one prays it alone.

Try it yourself. Repeat the Lord's Prayer replacing every "our," "us," and "we" with "my," "me," and "I." Do you not immediately sense how self-centered the words become? Does not the prayer feel suddenly restricting? Jesus constructed his prayer using the plural because that is who we are as his followers and that is how we live—we are plural. We are community.

If we pray when we're alone, interweaving our personal prayer with the Lord's Prayer, and we pray, for example, about a heavy grief that envelops us, then we pray also, inevitably, for others who know grief at the same moment as we do. We are not entirely by ourselves, whatever we are feeling. And those others are not entirely by themselves either, whatever they're doing. We're all in this together.

Our hurts, our fears, our regrets, our sorrows—these unite us as children of God, just as do our joys, our loves, our serendipities, our gratitudes. Once we pray "our Father," we can no longer pray in a fenced-in way, looking out only for ourselves.

One more issue confronts us in these first words of address, an issue that is a sticking point for some more than others. Jesus said *abba*. He did not say *imma*, the Aramaic word for "mother," and there is no Aramaic word that expresses a close, personal relationship with a parent that suits either gender. Nor is there in Greek. Nor is there in English.

It is undoubtedly true that the language we use can easily and even unknowingly influence our minds. It's true that the use of masculine nouns and pronouns can suggest the presence of paternalism in our thinking. It's true that, for some, any reference to

God in father language can bring to mind uncomfortable memories and undeniable hurts.

So what are we to do? Some choose to alternate "Mother" and "Father" as they pray, or they use both terms, in the full awareness of the mothering essence of this God that Jesus spoke about and told parables about. Some people do all they can to remove all gender references to God, simply saying "God" or "God's" at every turn, since God is, of course, *beyond* all gender.

What it comes down to is this: the absolute essence of God confounds human language. If we speak of God, and if we address God in prayer, we are almost inevitably, eventually led to use analogy, as imperfect as that is. The analogy that Jesus used is *abba*.

I believe the gospel record at every point shows that Jesus held women in equal regard to men before God. I do not believe he intended to limit God to a masculine identity. I believe he wanted to enlarge people's understandings of who God is and how God acts. God is love, in an active form. God exists for relationship, beyond all human equivalences. And to express that truth Jesus chose a warm, personal form of address: *abba*. It was the best he knew to do in that part of the world at that time in history. So the Lord's Prayer is the Abba Prayer.

Be the child.

Repeat the Lord's Prayer unhurriedly. At the end of every short phrase say, "Abba," as if you're speaking to God as a trusting child. When you're done, wait in silence in case God has anything God wants you to know.

A short prayer pierces the heavens.

JOHN OF THE CROSS

Teach us to pray often,
that we may pray oftener.

JEREMY TAYLOR

We must remember that the business of prayer
does not consist in thinking much,
but in loving much. Do, therefore,
whatever may excite you most to love.

TERESA OF ÁVILA

And one called to another and said:
"Holy, holy, holy is the Lord of hosts;
the whole earth is full of his glory."

ISAIAH 6:3

Whatever else we say when we pray,
if we pray as we should,
we are only saying what is already contained
in the Lord's Prayer.

AUGUSTINE OF HIPPO

Name

The story has been told too many times, but I'll tell it again anyway because of two points it makes.

The boy lies in bed and his mother sits beside him, ready for the ritual of his nightly prayer. He begins, "Harold, bless mommy and daddy, bless—". His mother interrupts. "Did you just call God 'Harold'?" "Yes," he says, "I learned that from you. I heard you praying, 'Our Father who art in heaven, Harold be thy name."

The boy in the story, in all his innocence, is not unlike many of us, in stories of our own prayer lives. This phrase, "hallowed be thy name," *is* an unusual one. The words sound strange on our lips. The concept is challenging to our minds.

Hallowed. According to one study, 17,101 different English words are used more frequently than this one. Much more popular synonyms are *holy* and *sacred*. But our gospel translations go with the word based on the verb *to hallow*, which means to honor as holy.

The Aramaic word which Jesus probably used, *qadash*, is rooted in the image of a person leaning over an area on the ground and clearing it, sweeping it clean, so it can be prepared for a special use. Hallowing involves a setting apart.

Over time the idea developed that other things could be set apart as holy too—not just certain places, but certain people, certain times, certain objects. In the prayer that Jesus composed, it was a name that was to be sanctified—in this case, *thy* name.

The name, of course, means God's name. Saying *thy name* was a way of saying *God* without pronouncing aloud that extremely sacred word. Yet this name was much more than just a name. As one theologian explained, "The name of God stands for the whole being of God. To know God's name is to know God's character, God's personality, God's love, God's mercy, God's power."

"Hallowed be thy name," therefore, really means, "Hallowed be thy true Essence, O God, thy truest Being."

A second way our own innocence may overlap that of the boy saying his prayers relates to how the first sentence of the Lord's Prayer is often spoken: "Our Father who art in heaven, [short pause after the comma] hallowed be thy name. [longer pause after the period]" Spoken in this way, these first ten words form a whole sentence. Pronounced aloud they easily come across as, and are treated as, "Our Father who art in heaven, hallowed *is* (or *equals*) thy name."

But that is not at all the way this prayer begins. It is not a declarative sentence. These first words form a petition, a request, an appeal. "May it happen that thy name is actively, properly hallowed." "May it come to be that thy name, thy purest Divine Essence, is truly lifted up as holy for all to see." These words carry with them a deep urge, a strong yearning. This sentence does more than just state—it begs. "Oh, may it be that this will indeed happen! And now!"

Who is it then who hallows this name? *We* do, we who say the prayer. It's up to us. If God is going to be set apart as the One who, above all others, is absolutely sacred, then we are the ones who must do the setting apart, the hallowing.

If we believe God to be the Creator of the Universe, then how do we show our reverence for God and for God's holy creation? How do we show our sacred respect for this created-out-nothing earth? How do we show reverence for all that is in and on it, for all that surrounds it? If we believe that the image of God has been placed upon every human being, as it states in Genesis, then what does that say about how we are to treat all those around us, day in, day out?

Standing before an overcrowded room of anxious people in a bombed-out Stuttgart in 1944, the German theologian Helmut Thielicke spoke words that echo yet today:

"My friends, if Jesus does not teach us to pray, 'Make *me* a consecrated, holy person,' but rather teaches us to say, 'Hallowed be *thy* name,' what he is saying is this: 'Everything depends on your being willing to honor *God* and let *God* work in your life—simply to stand still and let God be the 'holy one' who will actually have first place in your life. *Then the other will come of itself.*'"

After we do our own hallowing of God with our daily words and actions, then we become, partially at least, hallowed ourselves, though that is not at all why we do what we do.

This is what it means to pray the first petition: "May thy name, thy Divine Presence, be hallowed and may I play my humble part in that hallowing."

Pray guerrilla style.

Select a stranger sitting near you in a waiting room, or standing in line at the store, or waiting at the stoplight, or anywhere at all. Pray the Lord's Prayer just for them. Then smile at them and move on.

Most people like short prayers and long sausages.

GERMAN PROVERB

Before we pray, "Lord, thy Kingdom come,"
we must be willing to pray, "My kingdom go."

ALAN REDPATH

As often as you can,
take a trip out to the fields to pray.
All the grasses will join you.
They will enter your prayers and give you strength
to sing praises to God.

NACHMAN OF BRESLOV

In this crazy world, there's an enormous distinction
between good times and bad, between sorrow and joy.
But in the eyes of God, they're never separated.
Where there is pain, there is healing.
Where there is mourning, there is dancing.
Where there is poverty, there is the Kingdom.

HENRI J. M. NOUWEN

Kingdom

When Jesus composed his prayer, he created it in two halves, each containing three petitions. These first petitions refer especially to God. The ostensible focus on the Divine will change in the second set of petitions.

Right in the middle of the prayer's first half we find "Thy kingdom come." Let us note two things that Jesus has done here.

He wanted his prayer to be easy to repeat. So the first petition has only two words in Aramaic. The first means "hallowed be" and the second, "thy name." Single letters from the Aramaic alphabet are often attached to individual words to supply additional meaning, with the result that it can require multiple English words to translate a single Aramaic one.

The second petition contains only two words as well: one meaning "may it come" followed by one meaning "thy kingdom." The main part of the third petition is also only two words long: the verb "may it be done" placed before the noun "thy will." Jesus wanted his prayer to be short and sweet.

The second fact is that Jesus provided an aid to help people remember his prayer. The three petitions rhyme in the language he and his followers spoke, all the better to commit his choice of words to memory.

Let us look more closely now at this second petition: "May it come, thy kingdom." In the New Testament this is sometimes called the kingdom of God, sometimes the kingdom of heaven, sometimes just the kingdom. Jesus spoke of this kingdom ninety times in the gospels—no other subject commanded as much attention from him. "The time is fulfilled and the kingdom of God is at hand," he said. "Truly, I say to you, unless one is born again one cannot see the kingdom of God."

The kingdom was the subject of many of his parables, as he compared it to a tiny mustard seed that could grow into a great tree, or a small amount of yeast that can leaven an entire loaf.

Looking at the language Jesus used and the parables he told, I believe it's unfortunate that our word kingdom has been chosen so often to translate the Aramaic word Jesus used, *malkutakh*, and the Greek word the gospel writers used, *basileia*. In both cases there is no reference to anything kingly. In fact, both of these two words connote the feminine as readily as the masculine. Moreover, our idea of kingdom easily evokes images of geographic terrain and circumscribed borders.

A more accurate translation would be "the realm of God" or perhaps "the time of God." What Jesus described is an event more than a place, a way of living in the world that includes God's sure presence rather than a place with streets paved in gold.

When we pray "Thy kingdom come," we're petitioning that the realm in which God operates may become as vast and as expansive, as clear and as full of light, as humankind can experience. It will know no boundaries. Ultimately, this will be the Realm of Love, encompassing all the earth, all creatures, all peoples.

How will this come to be? The Biblical scholar John Dominic Crossan says that the notion of God's coming is not so much about the immanence of divine intervention, as about the empowerment of human collaboration. God can't do this alone. Nor can we humans do it alone. We must be together.

Before, during, and after Jesus devoted the last years of his life on earth preaching, teaching, and healing, many held on to the expectation that the coming of this new realm would be swift, sudden, and dramatic. That, of course, did not happen. So where does that leave us today, we who still regularly pray, "May thy kingdom come"? What is our role as imperfect, limited human beings?

One answer comes from Evelyn Underhill, the English spiritual writer, who penned in her meditation on this second petition that we have a responsibility with our whole use of created things, including our money, our position, our politics, and the papers we read. She said, "Each act of love, each sacrifice, each conquest of prejudice, each generous impulse carried through into action counts."

Similarily, Rowan Williams, Archbishop of Canterbury, said in an interview, "Jesus himself tells us that the kingdom comes in unexpected ways; it doesn't just come with a clap of thunder at the end of time. It grows in our midst secretly. It comes through in quirky little moments when people do extraordinary things, take extraordinary risks, and you think, *ah, yes, that's a life in which God is showing through.*"

That's what this petition of the Lord's Prayer yearns for: more and more quirky moments when people do extraordinary things, sometimes in very ordinary ways—people like you and I.

Look admiringly.

Find a place in nature and pray the Lord's Prayer with your eyes wide open, as often as you wish. Or bring nature to you with a photograph. Pray with curious, appreciative, child-like, loving eyes. Smile. Do this often.

In God's will is our peace.

DANTE ALIGHIERI

The third clause of the Lord's Prayer
is repeated daily by millions
who have not the slightest intentions
of letting any will be done except their own.

ALDOUS HUXLEY

Help me to serve only Thy purposes,
to speak and write only Thy words,
to think only Thy thoughts,
to have no other prayer than "Thy will be done."

MALCOLM MUGGERIDGE

Walk and talk and work and laugh with your friends.
But behind the scenes, keep up the life
of simple prayer and inward worship.
Keep it up throughout the day.
Let inward prayer be your last act before you fall asleep
and the first act when you awake.

THOMAS R. KELLY

Will

"Thy will be done" is the third and last "thou" petition. It's different from the first two.

First, there's that phrase at the end: "on earth as it is in heaven," or, as originally written in the Greek, "as in heaven, so upon earth." Something is one way in the domain of God that exists beyond all space and all time—in heaven. Whatever that way is, this prayer calls for it to operate in the same way on earth.

In addition, God's will, unlike God's name and God's kingdom, is rooted in an active, personal intention to make something happen. For example, we might say of someone, "She willed herself to keep going." Or, in the context of the Judeo-Christian faith, for example, "God wills peace."

The Aramaic word for this will carries with it a strong sense of feeling, an ardent desire. Applying a human metaphor, God's will involves more than God's mind—it is driven equally by God's heart. God is deeply invested in this.

What is it that God wills? Ultimately, what is best for the universe that God has created. God wills love and compassion, because that's God's nature. God wills justice, but no more than forgiveness. God wills human freedom, but no more than human responsibility. God first willed, and always wills, beauty, every step of the way.

Yet this must also be said: God's will is not always obvious in given situations. It can be mysterious. But it is never capricious. It always moves in the direction of ultimate goodness.

Of course, we human beings have our own wills, if we're at all engaged in life. We wish for things to happen in certain ways, maybe at certain times, maybe for certain people, including, not least, ourselves. We can be very determined about how we want life to unfold.

So when we pray regularly, "May thy will be done," where does that leave the usually unspoken thought, "May my will be done too"?

Dom Hélder Cámara, the Brazilian Catholic archbishop, once said, "You know the prayer I love to say? 'Lord, may Your grace help me to want what You want, to prefer what You prefer.'" That's a good starting point for all of us—to fashion our own wills with a self-awareness that takes into account the possibility that another will, a larger will, has an idea or two. We check our own impulses before going too far with them.

The American mystic, Rufus Moseley, was fond of offering this perspective: "We must always pray and then say, or silently desire, 'Lord, this is the best I can think of in the situation. But if You have something better in mind, then cancel my prayer and give us Yours!'"

If God's will is going to be done, then sometimes we must cancel or alter our own wills, no matter how well-intentioned and sincere they may be. Sometimes we must prepare to follow God's will, even if it doesn't feel right as we begin, even if we cannot be sure exactly where we're being led. This is not easy stuff. At the least, it requires of us a great deal of patience. It can require real courage, even heroism.

The University of Chicago theologian Martin Marty says that we dare not speak "Thy will be done" simply as a prayer of resignation, submissively abandoning an important part of who we are. Instead, he advocates that we turn "Thy will be done" into a different kind of prayer—a battle cry, as we move to make God's will real on earth. We do this right here, right now, bringing heaven into closer contact with this amazing, struggling, beautiful, yet ever so broken earth. And if we are not the ones who take up this cry, then who will?

With the conclusion of this third petition, the prayer that Jesus taught makes an abrupt transition. After expressing the loftiest faith in God, the focus turns to the living of the ordinary days of those who make use of this prayer. By placing these two strands together, the truly holy and the truly human, Jesus wants us to know that our everyday lives demand our equal attention, our equal work. Let's turn now to see what he wants us to pray next.

Pray as if your arm were around.

Think of someone who deserves a prayer. Then speak the Lord's Prayer especially for them. At every "we" or "us," say their name or use the appropriate pronoun. Add your own prayer for them at the end. You need not tell them.

Lord, make us mindful of the little things
that grow and blossom in these days
to make the world beautiful for us.

W. E. B. DuBois

The best things are nearest: breath in your nostrils,
light in your eyes, flowers at your feet,
duties at your hand, the path of God just before you.
Then do not grasp at the stars,
but do life's plain common work as it comes,
certain that daily duties and daily bread
are the sweetest things in life.

Robert Louis Stevenson

There is no such thing as "my" bread.
All bread is ours and is given to me,
to others through me and to me through others.
For not only bread but all things necessary
for sustenance in this life are given on loan
to us with others, and because of others
and for others and to others through us.

Meister Eckhart

Bread

The fourth petition has been waiting in the wings, ready to usher us in an entirely new direction. There is not a "thy" in sight. Now it's all about "we" and "us" and "ours." The two-worded petitions give way to longer ones. And for reasons that have nothing to do with their length, each of the next three petitions presents a translation problem.

"Give us this day our daily bread."

The problem word here is *epiousios*, as in "*epiousios* bread." What's the problem, you might ask, except that it's a Greek word I don't know the meaning of? That's the problem. It's the Greek word in the very first manuscripts of Matthew's gospel that *no one* knows the meaning of—not then, not now. This word appears only two times in the Bible—here and in Luke's version of the Lord's Prayer. It's recorded in no Greek literature anywhere at all.

This is probably what happened: Jesus associated an Aramaic word with the word for bread, a word that had no Greek equivalent. So the Jewish translator coined his own word that he thought approximated the Aramaic, and hoped it would make sense. It didn't.

Through the centuries scholars have written hundreds if not thousands of pages, making their arguments for the true meaning. Rather than add our voice to the continuing debate, we'll take the easy way out and go with the most popular translation: "daily bread." Besides, it's the one that makes the most sense.

The other words in this petition are straightforward: "Give to us our daily bread today, please." Jesus up until this point had focused on God's splendor; now he turns his attention to human concerns.

Jesus speaks about, blesses, and handles bread a surprising number of times in the gospels. Bread was a central element in a Palestinian's diet, baked at home in small clay ovens, heated by burning wood and dried grass. The loaves were small, rounded, and flat. They were an essential part of every meal.

When Jesus suggests that his followers pray to receive their daily bread, he acknowledges their truth—without bread, these people could not live. Bread prepared the way they baked it could not last long, so they had to bake it fresh every morning. (Of course, they had to grow the wheat and barley, and harvest it, and grind it, and mix the dough, and knead it, too.)

Over the course of time, the word "bread" came to stand for the entire meal, so "the breaking of bread" (they broke their bread apart, never cutting it) came to mean "sharing a meal together." And did Jesus ever break bread with others! Care was taken to describe him dining in friends' homes, with outcastes, among his disciples wherever they went, on hillsides with thousands reclining on the grass. Meals with Jesus had a way of becoming banquets, using the most common of elements—a few fish, a handful of loaves. In this simple act, he created an atmosphere that gave expression to the hallowing of everyday life. As the German theologian Joachim Jeremias once explained, "The bread which he proffered when he sat at table with publicans and sinners was everyday bread, and yet it was more: it was the bread of life. Every meal his disciples had with him was a usual eating and drinking, and was more: a meal of salvation, a messianic meal. The same remained true in the primitive church: their daily fellowship meals were the customary meals for sustenance, and yet at the same time they were a 'Lord's Supper.'"

Asking for daily bread was, I believe, an affirmation that the small things in life are important, not just to humans but to God. But even more, it created an opening for this daily hallowing of life which Jesus modeled, finding the sacred in the commonplace, touching the eternal in shared times of momentary experiences. By his direction and his example, food for the body could also be accompanied by food for the soul. Any day. Every day.

One more truth begs for our attention. In having the petition read, "Give *us* this day *our* daily bread," Jesus led people to realize that ultimately "us" means *all* of us—those who have plenty and those who know poverty, those who have enough to eat and those who go hungry, children as well as adults. *Our* daily bread means the regular physical sustenance that every human being deserves and has the right to. Understood in this way, the Lord's Prayer has a forceful, even revolutionary, thrust to it. If our daily bread belongs to *all* of us, then what will it take for *all* of us to have it, to eat it, to be nourished by it, daily?

Who would have thought that prayer could be a subversive activity?

Pray for or with someone you love.

Recite the Lord's Prayer with your dear one in mind. Better, say it aloud with them, perhaps hand in hand or arms over shoulders. Then silently touch your foreheads together in gratitude. Carry that memory through the coming day, and night.

The heart has always the pardoning power.

ANNE SOPHIE SWETCHINE

God pardons like a mother,
who kisses the offense into everlasting forgiveness.

HENRY WARD BEECHER

We should always forgive.
We should forgive the repentant for their sake,
the unrepentant for our sake.

MARIE VON EBNER-ESCHENBACH

O eternal God, let me, in spite of me,
be of so much use to your glory,
that by your mercy and my sin,
other sinners may see how much sin you can pardon.

JOHN DONNE

Debts

Each Sunday the church I attend repeats the fifth petition of the Lord's Prayer this way: "Forgive us our debts, as we forgive our debtors." All the congregations I attended for the previous fifty years prayed, "Forgive us our trespasses, as we forgive those who trespass against us." The church my family belonged to when I was a child used a still different wording: "Forgive us our sins, as we forgive those who sin against us."

What gives? Blame this discrepancy, at least partially, on William and Miles.

In the original Aramaic, the most common word for "sin" was the same word that meant "debt." When Matthew's gospel was first written, in the language that was becoming increasingly popular, Greek, the word for "debt" was applied, even though "sin" was the original meaning.

William Tyndale, the British scholar who in 1525 first translated the entire Bible into English, chose, for reasons not entirely clear, to use the word "trespass" instead. Five hundred years ago that word did carry the connotation of "an offense," though it no longer does.

Ten years later another British church reformer came out with his translation. Miles Coverdale went with the word "debt," which is closer to the Aramaic. But behind both of these words lies the simpler and stronger and truer word: "sin." However much we may dislike using that word, it holds unquestioned truth for us. As human beings, we sometimes do wrong. We commit offenses. We misbehave. We transgress. We sin.

Instead of being truthful, we lie. Instead of treating all others kindly and respectfully, we can be known to treat them *unkindly, unfairly, unlovingly*. Much as we wish otherwise, we can act with jealousy, we can speak with uncalled-for anger or resentment, we can see through eyes that are filled with selfishness or ignorance. It happens to all of us—such things and even much worse. No one is immune.

So what are we to do? Uncomfortable as it feels, what's called for is to admit what we have done—to own it, to confess it. That means, first of all, to admit it to ourselves. That's the most crucial step for us to take, and often the most difficult.

We would like to avoid the fact that our temper got away from us, or that our prejudice got the best of us, or that our pettiness got in the way of our acting maturely. Most of us do not like to think that we could have been the source of cruel words or the cause of vengeful hurts or the originator of neglectful behavior. We may pretend, at least for a while, that we did not such thing. We may justify. We may rationalize. We may just plain deny the truth.

But if things are going to be set right again—with others, with our better selves—then we must acknowledge within that we have fallen short, causing a different sort of pain. Yet it is the *right* sort, the *helpful* sort, because it is the start of something positive.

An appropriate next step is to admit what we have done to whomever we have hurt. If that's not possible, then perhaps we can disclose our regret to someone we trust, realizing their role is not to give us an easy out, but for them to listen to us, believe in us, and help us visualize a way forward.

Always, of course, is the surest option of all: to take our confession to God, known to us as *Abba*. This can be how the most significant healing proceeds to take place.

Then, after all this, we ask for forgiveness.

The visual image lying behind the Aramaic word for "sin" involves an object that has gotten all knotted up, like a piece of yarn or a cord. That's not the way it's supposed to be, the way it originally was. It's all wrong. It's a mess. So Jesus taught us to pray, in essence, "May there be an unknotting of this awful knot we've created. May there be a straightening out of this terrible mess we've caused."

We cannot take back what we've done—it's right there for us to see, to wish it had never happened. But maybe, just maybe, we can be forgiven. Jesus says, in effect, "I believe you can be. Go ahead and ask. See what happens to that knottedness."

Augustine of Hippo, the Christian bishop from North Africa, took the Lord's Prayer as a favorite preaching topic. He was known to say that Christians are given complete forgiveness through the waters of their baptism as a once-for-all-time event. After that they are washed daily when they pray for forgiveness in what he called "the Holy Prayer." Augustine proposed a regular cleansing, made possible by the heartfelt praying of the fifth petition.

Jesus began this petition with "Forgive us our sins," and then he tacked on, "as we forgive those who sin against us." This is the only time in the Lord's Prayer that whoever is praying commits to an action that backs up the petition that has just been prayed. "Please forgive, and we will forgive too." We will forgive those who lie to us, who treat us wrongly, who injure us unfairly, who cause us pain.

We know, at least intellectually, that God forgives and that forgiveness is naturally an important part of God's repertoire. But how do we make it a part of *our* repertoire?

Three words were spoken on June 19, 2015 in Charleston, South Carolina that sparked a public debate that continues still. It was two days after Dylann Roof, a young, hate-filled, white man joined a Bible study group at Emanuel AME Church and at one point stood and proceeded to kill the dynamic pastor, Rev. Clemente Pinckney, and eight other African-Americans. At a bond hearing for the shooter, Nadine Collier, whose mother had been one of those gunned down, said three words to Dylann Roof: "I forgive you." Facing him she said, "You hurt me. You hurt a lot of people. But if God forgives you, I forgive you."

I wondered then and I wonder now if I could have spoken such words if my mother had been killed just forty-eight hours earlier. I doubt I could have. It was so soon! And that offense was so huge!

I read an article about Nadine on the one-year anniversary of those deaths. She still stood by her words but acknowledged what a challenge it was to truly forgive. Such forgiveness, if it's to be genuine, is not something you do nonchalantly. It is a huge undertaking. It is not a one-time event—it happens over and over.

And so it is with us. When we forgive another, or others, who have hurt us, we dare not do it unthinkingly, automatically. It requires a willingness to choose an action that is the opposite of our natural impulses. Such forgiveness requires clear determination and real inner strength. Forgiving others asks of us a maturity, a compassion, and eventually a readiness to let go of what we don't have to let go of. There are reasons not to let go! But we choose another way: "Forgive us our mighty failures, as we forgive those who fail us mightily."

This forgiveness business is not all sweetness and light. It addition to the effort it takes, and even the repeated effort, our act of forgiving may not go exactly as we wish.

The other person may not be aware of our forgiveness. We forgive anyway. The other person may not want or acknowledge or accept our forgiveness. We forgive anyway. The other person may not change their ways. We forgive anyway.

We forgive because it is the right thing to do. We forgive because if we do not, eventually we will be the ones who are harmed by our non-forgiveness—it will remain a burden upon us. Remaining unforgiving will require of us a psychological and spiritual energy to keep hanging on to this wrong that has been done to us—energy that could be expended in more constructive ways.

But mostly we forgive because it is the Christian thing to do, and because Jesus made that plain in the prayer he composed for us. Ultimately, we forgive because we have a model to follow: *Abba* forgives us, ever so freely, ever so lovingly. We will always do well to remember that, and then follow along.

Pray for that difficult person.

Who has offended you or hurt you or angered you? Maybe it's someone close or someone you barely know, except you know what they stand for. Pray the Lord's Prayer for them, inserting their name. Then breathe deeply and peacefully.

The best prayers often have more groans than words.

JOHN BUNYAN

Trouble and perplexity drive me to prayer
and prayer drives away perplexity and trouble.

PHILIP MELANCHTHON

O, do not pray for easy lives.
Pray to be stronger people.
Do not pray for tasks equal to your powers.
Pray for powers equal to your tasks.

PHILLIPS BROOKS

In Gethsemane the holiest of all petitioners
prayed three times that a certain cup might pass from him.
It did not.
After that the idea that prayer is recommended to us
as a sort of infallible gimmick may be dismissed.

C. S. LEWIS

Temptation

It's not every day that the Lord's Prayer makes headline news. That's exactly what happened December 8, 2017. In its worldwide broadcast, BBC News led off with this teaser: "Lord's Prayer: Pope Francis Calls for Change."

In an interview on Italian TV, the pontiff had said, "'Lead us not into temptation' is not a good translation, because God does not cause humans to sin." He said better wording would be, "Do not let us fall into temptation." The pope explained, "It is I who falls. It is not God who throws me into temptation and then sees how I fell. A father does not do that. A father helps you get up immediately."

Pope Francis is correct. "Lead us not into temptation" is not the best of translations.

Our English word "temptation" means "the desire to do something, especially something unwise or wrong." It often smacks of luridness. One can hear the sound of people clucking their tongues. But the word in Aramaic, and in Greek, carries much more the idea of "a time of trial" or "a time of testing," with more neutral undertones.

The other part of the phrase we have been given to use, "do not lead us," is decidedly not true to the original meaning. More accurate translations might be "may we not fall into" or "may we not venture into." It's not a matter of someone steering us in a certain direction. Instead we know the choice is ours and we're seeking support in making the good choice, the healthy choice, rather than the tempting choice.

These trials and temptations can come in a myriad of forms, more than we might imagine, and these can vary from person to person. I am personally not tempted at all to experiment with illicit drugs, but I am tempted to buy and experiment with using large numbers of the latest Apple products regardless of whether I need them or not. Who am I to look askance at another?

In praying this sixth petition, we're asking for help with those trials and temptations that keep us from living lives that do not honor our faith, our Master, or our God. We may not be good at deciding wisely how we treat others, how we take care of ourselves, how we respect the world around us. We may make choices that are foolish, or reckless, or selfish, or all three. We may struggle with doing what's moral. Many do.

This last petition has a second half: "but deliver us from evil." Other good translations of this verb would be "please set us free from" or "loosen the hold of."

Evil, of course, is evil. It is a profound wickedness and depravity. It appears in all sorts of ways. The shooting of children in schools and adults in Bible study groups is evil. Genocide and ethnic cleansing are evil. Child abuse, elder abuse, and spousal abuse are evil. Racism and sexism and ageism are evil. We do not like to think that evil lurks around us, but it can, it does.

Some versions of the Lord's Prayer do not read "deliver us from evil" but "deliver us from the Evil One." I am not inclined to make a personal Devil a part of this prayer, or, for that matter, necessarily a part of the Christian faith. True evil is real enough without having a figure called Satan take responsibility for it. But I realize that many think otherwise, perhaps even with good reason. After all, it was Pope Francis who observed, right after saying that God does not toss us into temptation, "The one who leads us into temptation is Satan." Who am I to question the pope?

Whatever our belief system, the ultimate truth is that in our times of trial and temptation, and in our skirmishes with evil, we are never left alone. God is there with us. And we will know the reality of Julian of Norwich's words of assurance: "He said not 'Thou shalt not be tempested, thou shalt not be travailed, thou shalt not be dis-eased'; but he said, 'Thou shalt not be overcome.'"

Not yesterday, not today, not tomorrow. We have that on the best of Authority.

Pray in your own words.

Pause at the end of each line of the Lord's Prayer, restating it in your own words. Do this two or three times if you wish, using different words each time, as you get closer and closer to its meaning for your life.

God is like a person who clears his throat
while hiding and so gives himself away.

MEISTER ECKHART

Let no one deify the universe;
rather let us seek after the Creator of the Universe.

CLEMENT OF ALEXANDRIA

The whole world is charged with the glory of God
and I feel fire and music under my feet.

THOMAS MERTON

While Einstein's theory of relativity may one day
put Earth on the intergalactic map,
it will always run a distant second to the Lord's Prayer,
whose harnessing of energies in their proper,
life-giving direction surpasses even the discovery of fire.

KURT VONNEGUT

Glory

"For thine is the kingdom and the power and the glory forever." This final phrase of the Lord's Prayer is not in the earliest manuscripts of The Gospel According to Matthew. It's certain that Jesus did not compose these words as the ending that we have come to know.

While Jesus's prayer appears to screech to an abrupt end with the word "evil," the Biblical scholar Joachim Jeremias explains that in Palestinian Judaism something called a seal was commonly used as a conclusion to most prayers. This seal was a sentence of praise to God, spoken by the one doing the praying. It could be simple and impromptu, such as "Praises be to God." Or it could be longer and composed of more formal language.

Near the end of his life, just before turning over his throne to his son, Solomon, King David spoke his own praises in his farewell prayer this way: "Thine, O Lord, is the greatness, and the power, and the glory, and the victory, and the majesty, for all that is in the heavens and in the earth is thine; thine is the kingdom...." We cannot help but notice the similarities, can we?

The final phrase of the Lord's Prayer is called its doxology, a word that in its original Greek means "saying or speaking of the glory." This particular wording was formalized during the second century as the Lord's Prayer increasingly became a regular part of services of worship. These dozen words constituted a fitting and grand finale, returning the theme to the prayer's beginnings—the first three petitions focusing on the Divine.

Here at the end, a three-fold exaltation of God's character is proclaimed: the kingdom, the power, and the glory. The amazing expanse of God's realm, reaching everywhere. The limitless potential of God's energy, flowing from the very beginning of time. And the astounding beauty and majesty of the Divine Presence, reflected throughout the expanding universe.

An early church leader named Clement of Alexandria, who did his most important work around 200 AD, once shared what he reported was a saying of Jesus that is not preserved in the gospels: "Ask great things, and small shall be added to you; ask heavenly things, and there shall be added unto you earthly things."

It appears that is what Jesus intended to communicate with this prayer. "Pray for the great things, like the hallowing of thy name, the coming of thy kingdom, and the doing of thy will," he says in effect, "and the smaller things will come as well—the daily bread, the forgiveness of common sins, the falling away of personal trials and temptations."

In the way he composed his prayer, Jesus seems to be communicating, "Build your prayers around more than just your small 'I.' Yes, it's reasonable to include your individual concerns and needs, but don't make those your only focus as you pray. Don't let those smaller things *govern* your prayer. Remember to pray for the great things too, always!"

Besides, we will do well to remember what Jesus said immediately before he first revealed the Lord's Prayer in Matthew's gospel: "Your Father knows what you need before you ask him."

There's one final word for us to recognize, of course: "amen." It has roots in both the Aramaic and Hebrew languages, as well as in Jewish, Christian, and Muslim worship. It's used as a concluding response to prayers. It means, "So be it!" It was spoken with feeling and considered to be a solemn oath. People would say "amen!" as a way of adding their personal assent to what had just been expressed. "Yes!" "Certainly so!" Or as some might say today, "I'm all in!"

Jesus was an amen-er himself. All those times in the gospels when what he said was translated as "truly, truly" and "verily"? The word he used was "amen!"

To which we add as this particular chapter concludes, "Amen indeed!"

Pray for the whole world.

Say the Lord's Prayer slowly, resolutely, hopefully, keeping the whole world in mind—all peoples, all nations, all religions. Pray each of the six petitions from this universal perspective. See what your praying leads you to do afterward.

Afterword

Prayer does not change God,
but it changes the one who prays.

SØREN KIERKEGAARD

A Christian has prayed abundantly
who has rightly prayed the Lord's Prayer.

MARTIN LUTHER

Don't try to reach God
with your understanding;
that is impossible.
Reach God in love;
that is possible.

CARLO CARRETTO

Proper praying is like a person
who wanders through a field gathering flowers—
one by one, until they make a beautiful bouquet.
In the same manner, a person must gather
each letter, each syllable, to form them
into words of prayer.

NACHMAN OF BRATSLOV

Personal Reflections

John Doberstein was the man entrusted to translate German theologian Helmut Thielicke's sermons on the Lord's Prayer into English. In the preface to that collection he referred to Martin Luther's famous quote, "The Lord's Prayer is the greatest martyr, for everyone tortures it and abuses it." Doberstein explained that the prayer has become so familiar that we are tempted to pray it mechanically and thoughtlessly.

When I am among a group of people reciting the Lord's Prayer, I sometimes have a desire, several seconds in, to interrupt and say, "Stop! Wait! How about a little vocal inflection here? Let's slow down and pay real attention to the specific words, the individual phrases! Let's *pray* this prayer and not just mouth it!"

I haven't interrupted yet. But there's always next Sunday....

I find myself deeply gratified that we have been given this prayer to call ours. (An aside here: some have called this the Disciples' Prayer since Jesus actually gave it to his disciples, all of us.) This masterful prayer gives us a direct link, a bond, to the man who so carefully composed the original words and put every part of the prayer in the order he wanted.

I believe it's possible, each time we speak it, to get a clearer sense of the wisdom, the depth, the heart, and the soul of the man from Nazareth. Underneath the flow of the words, the simplicity of the language, and the manner in which God is approached, something authentic emerges. A messianic spirit arises.

The Messiah appears. Jesus's eloquent prayer verifies who he genuinely was, and is.

❁

I wish we could all speak Aramaic. I wish we all could have been there to hear Jesus enunciate the Lord's Prayer the first time, if not many times after. Wouldn't it have been wonderfully fulfilling to repeat it with him after he had taught us all the words?

Understandably, the words we're given to use today are far removed from that first verbal giving. We have only translations to work from, some better than others, some closer to the original. In at least a couple of places in our version of the Lord's Prayer, we almost need to change a particular word or two in our minds if we're going to pray the thought that Jesus first expressed. Going from one language, through another, to still a third can be a delicate maneuver.

It's difficult to imagine that the beloved wording we've grown accustomed to might one day change. But perhaps it will. The first Sunday in Advent in 2017, the Catholic parishes in all of France changed the wording of the sixth petition, "Lead us not into temptation," to this in French: "Don't let us enter into temptation." As Emmanuel Schwab, pastor of a congregation in Paris, said, "The former language made people think that God threw banana peels in front of them to see if they would slip and fall." God, of course, would do not such thing. But the traditional language was somewhat ambiguous.

Perhaps in our lifetimes, or our children's, a slight alteration in a word or two here or there will help English-speaking Christians pray the Lord's Prayer without needing to make an adjustment in our minds as we do so.

When we pray the Lord's Prayer, we participate in an unbroken succession of these spoken and silent prayers, carried on innumerable languages, hosted on every land on earth, through twenty centuries of living, of dying, of loving, of hallowing. This prayer unites us with every Christian, living and deceased, well known and unknown, who has ever walked this planet and ever will. We are each an integral link in a long line of witnesses.

I sometimes wonder, "Did Jesus have any concept of how this short, simple, dense prayer would continue to speak so sensitively and so powerfully so many millennia later? Could he have known that afternoon on that Galilean hillside?"

Frederick Buechner, the Presbyterian minister and prolific author, offered this advice in one of his books: "Go where your best prayers take you."

Isn't that glorious guidance? Go where your truest prayers lead you. Follow in the direction that your most faith-filled and honest prayers point you.

Learn to trust where Jesus's prayer coaxes you, day after day, and see where your travels take you.

I believe you will not be disappointed.

Books by James E. Miller

When Mourning Dawns

A Pilgrimage Through Grief

How Will I Get Through the Holidays?

What Will Help Me?/How Can I Help?

One You Love Has Died

When a Man Faces Grief/A Man You Know Is Grieving

Winter Grief, Summer Grace

Autumn Wisdom

The Caregiver's Book

When You're Ill or Incapacitated/When You're the Caregiver

This Time of Caregiving

When You Know You're Dying

One You Love Is Dying

Change & Possibility

The Art of Being a Healing Presence

The Art of Listening in a Healing Way

The Gift of Healing Presence

My Shepherd Is the Lord

The Rewarding Practice of Journal Writing

and others

These books may be found at *www.willowgreen.com*.

Video Programs by James E. Miller

Invincible Summer

Listen to Your Sadness

How Do I Go On?

Common Bushes Afire

By the Waters of Babylon

Nothing Is Permanent Except Change

We Will Remember

Gaining a Heart of Wisdom

The Grit and Grace of Being a Caregiver

Awaken to Hope

Be at Peace

The Natural Way of Prayer

You Shall Not Be Overcome

When Mourning Dawns

All Seasons Shall Be Sweet

My Shepherd Is the Lord

Still Waters

The Art of Listening in a Healing Way

The Healing Promise of Grief

and others

These videos may be found at *www.willowgreen.com.*

James E. Miller is a graduate of DePauw University and holds advanced degrees from Garrett Theological Seminary and Garrett-Evangelical Theological Seminary. He planned upon a long career as a parish minister but he learned in early midlife that ministry can take forms one might not expect. For starters, a good friend introduced him to photography, which led him in new directions and extensive travels and to the collection of hundreds of thousands of images that he began to incorporate in his work. Having never intended to write a book of any sort, Jim ended up authoring twenty-five. He never imagined that he'd become the producer of his own videos designed to help others on their life journeys, yet several dozen mysteriously came into being.

Just as it takes a village to raise a child, it takes a fair-sized community to raise Jim Miller. That includes his wife, Bernie, and the families of their three children, as well as the members of the extended Miller clan, those on earth and those beyond earth. Jim has also been raised by a large gaggle of good friends, kind professionals, former parishioners, and the occasional reprobate.

He may be reached via email at *jmiller@willowgreen.com*. Samples of his work may be found at *www.willowgreen.com*.